# MARRIED & HAVING FUN!!!

DR. SHONDA KIRK & JOE KIRK JR.

Order this book online at www.trafford.com
or email orders@trafford.com

Most Trafford titles are also available at major online book retailers.

 **www.trafford.com**

**North America & international**
toll-free: 844 688 6899 (USA & Canada)
fax: 812 355 4082

Our mission is to efficiently provide the world's finest, most comprehensive book publishing service, enabling every author to experience success. To find out how to publish your book, your way, and have it available worldwide, visit us online at www.trafford.com

Because of the dynamic nature of the Internet, any web addresses or links contained in this book may have changed since publication and may no longer be valid. The views expressed in this work are solely those of the author and do not necessarily reflect the views of the publisher, and the publisher hereby disclaims any responsibility for them.

Any people depicted in stock imagery provided by Getty Images are models,
and such images are being used for illustrative purposes only.
Certain stock imagery © Getty Images.

ISBN: 978-1-6987-1168-3 (sc)
ISBN: 978-1-6987-1167-6 (e)

Print information available on the last page.

Trafford rev.04/06/2022

# CONTENTS

# HOW IT ALL STARTED

I want to share a little story with you. I was unhappy, divorced, wedlock mother and just tore up from the floor up, and God brought my J into my daughter's and my life, and everything changed.

Yeah, I was in a dysfunctional home growing up, boy was I messed up when my mother brought me to my grandmother. There was no hope for me. Life kinda gave me some bad blows, but because I went to a praying grandmother, life seemed to change for me. Have you ever wanted to be loved? This is what I needed. Love. Love, love. But I found it was not in growing up but in me loving me. My grandmother taught me a lot by her lifestyle. She loved God and my grandfather. Yes, she is a preacher. I adore and I thank God for her. So to be honest, after seeing my mother and father divorce for whatever reasons, but seeing my grandmother love my grandfather through all seasons, truly taught me marriage is a beautiful thing. I am saying people are not perfect, no one is, but in my eyes, my grandmother should get a trophy. She is truly a woman of God after God's heart who loves God and desires to do his will in her life. I have learn so much from her in the years I have observed her marriage and the ministry God has given her.

The joy of being married comes from knowing you are with your soul mate. When God put you together, the Bible says let no man separate you. I like to say don't let yourself separate your marriage. Since I have been married for more than twenty-two years, I have learned a lot about marriage. Two parties need to have the same mind, and goals must be in agreement. Sometimes we meet people, and we expect the man or woman to automatically know what is on our minds. I would like to say when you are preparing to get married, the first thing you have to make sure is your goals are in the same direction.

You cannot say you love God, and they don't love God but love the world. This is being unequally yoked, and this could destroy your marriage before you get married. Unity is found in two people who walk together and agree. Do you agree you need to go to church? Do you agree you need to live with one man or one woman? Share these types of questions with your future spouse beforehand.

It amazing how we expect something out of a relationship we never have shared, and when it is not given, we get upset. Why? Because we want to receive something that was never voiced. A relationship built on trust and communication cannot be stopped. The only reason marriage fails is when one party decides it is not working together. I can imagine God, Jesus, and the Holy Spirit in heaven arguing who will pray, where they will have dinner, when will they have children. Yes, these are some of the issues families deal with because of lack of communication. It becomes blown up and a big volcano that is overflowing with hot anger.

If I could share with you the times I failed in communication and became isolated, it was because of ignorance. I almost shipwrecked my marriage in the '90s. It was love at first death, not love at first sight. It took me to be dying of myself, yes, laying down my pride and wanting change. Change is not change until we change. We can talk the talk all we want and never walk the walk. Marriage is not built on one person. It is built on each other. The best way to know your mate is to forgive your mate for all things they may do, but also it teaches a lesson in the marriage of love. Love is forgiveness. My husband has the most forgiving heart. Since we are pastors and been married, since we have been pastoring, he sees the best in people. He balances our marriage and our ministry in Life Changers International Ministries. It is a joy to stand beside him daily and do the work of the Lord. I thank God because as we walk together and agree, more grace has come upon our lives. Please never think marriage is easy, it may not be easy, but it is worth investing in. The joy of being married is knowing two beings, two minds together and desire to do more together than apart.

As we can see in our churches, there is such a high divorce rate. My husband and I desire to help change that statistic. It is vital as Godly examples to make sure we share our experience about our marriage. We would like for you to enjoy this book and take something with you that will change your life for the rest of your life.

May God grant you insight on the pitfalls that have plagued so many people's marriage and cause change in your life. Marriage is God's way, and this is the right way!

# HE CAN'T HEAR

Have you ever heard the saying, "Men have selective hearing"? This may be the funniest chapter you'll read in this entire book. I was at the knowledge after getting married to my wonderful husband, Joe Kirk Jr., he could hear very well. I mean he was a marine, and a marine hears well and follows orders. Well, that was not in my case. Over the years, I began to see my husband would hear some things but not other things, so at first, I thought it was me. The first years of marriage—woooooo—was hell. It was not that he could not hear me. It was that I was a problem child—rebellious, stubborn, and downright nasty—but he could hear me. He responded to everything that I said. I would like to say with love. I think my other marriage really messed me up. Yes, I am a divorcee, and I am not proud of it, but I did make a mistake, *church people*. I do not have it together and never have. I love the Lord but had some problems on the inside. My husband helped me through. Oh my, he heard me loud and clear, not by his own will. This was like our first five years of marriage. Everything seemed important that I spoke, although I was snobbish and nasty. LOL.

Years passing, I noticed I had to repeat or say, "Do you hear me?"

You know, this kind of ticked me off because as you know, ladies, we like to talk, but men are not like that. At least my man is not. Joe is a sweet man, he loves God, but there are times he be like, "What you say?" and y'all, that sentence belong to the point I don't want to repeat myself.

May I say this to you: Men have selective hearing. You know how I know? Because he answers me when I speak of golfing, football, or going out to eat. LOL. I was like, let me test the spirit by the spirit to see if this is from God. I found out it was not of God. Yes, it was like a blur of some type, or maybe his mind stopped and decided not to listen. I began to ask people who have been married a while about this, and they said it comes with years. It was a good thing for me. So guess what I did? I used sticking notes, messages on our iPhones, e-mails, etc. Whatever it took, I made it happen, and it began to get better.

Ladies, a key when he can't hear: start to pray like, "Lord, please have him be attentive to his ear." Remember this in marriage: You must communicate, and communication is the key to success. One of my mentors used to tell me no conversation, no resolution to your problem, and it gets more challenging. When a man does not communicate, they are shutting down in some way, especially when it comes to several days of this. Never allow your marriage to be a place of silence. Get the counseling you need and make it happen. Many of you may say, "He does not hear me."

This may be true. Check his ears. Talk to him about the situation. Do your part, ladies, but don't expect God to just put a magic touch on your marriage and you are not willing to do anything. It takes two people of the same mind to make a marriage work. A marriage should be based on the principles of God, and the Bible lets us know that marriage is from God. In the book of Genesis, we were made to multiply, and this is not just children but also in our relationship as husband and wife. He hears you, lady, but are you doing your part?

# DRESS CODE

This will be a chapter that is going to get your attention on marriage. How can we say we love each other but cannot dress in a way our companion may need us to dress? God does not want you, of course, to be walking around naked, but he does want you and your mate to enjoy each other. The dress code should be in a way that is decent. Now because we live in a naked world, we must understand that we cannot be like the world. The world is filled with so many things that would cause our dress code to be a blessing to it. The dress code of the Lord is pure and holy, and he wants us to be pleasing to our mate, but it's when we do things that are not of God in our dress code. A lot of people will throw what I am saying around and not receive it, but the way you dress is the way people receive you. It does not matter where you are from or who you are married to. We must make up in our minds we must be who God wants us to be, but that does not mean loving and have fun with you spouse.

You may be asking yourself if you should wear a certain type of clothing when you are a believer. I will say this: Enjoy what you wear with your spouse, but don't worship it. The moment you worship your clothes is the moment God will then cause you to see who you really are. My dress code is decent for the kingdom and decent to the needs of my husband. I remember when my husband was dating me, he was buying me all this Liz Claiborne type of wear. The clothing line was cute, and so when I got married, I wanted the same upkeep. Well, of course, we purchased cars and a home, and we could not at first afford. A lot of the things change when you have children and have more bills than you can handle. My dress code for Jesus never changed because I always had him as my foundation.

As far as being married, you can be sexy and love the Lord. I love the Lord, and I also love my husband. My husband likes legs. LOL. He loves it when I show my legs. My legs are not your ordinary legs, but they are short and with muscles and light skin. Now I know y'all religious folks. The first thing you'll say is "God is not in that." Okay! That is your opinion. My husband is not telling me to sin and not wanting me to sin. He is just asking for a new dress code on particular nights. I would like all the ladies who read this book to know you can be sexy and enjoy the goodness of God. I can enjoy being who my husband wants me to be without sinning and still love the Lord with all my mind, heart, and soul. I believe God wants us to be a loving, attractive, joyous, sexually-pleasing mate to our spouse. When we are not this way, it causes us to be stuck on religion or tradition. Marriage and having fun is not what we think it is. It is what is needed for your mate to enjoy you. In marriage, you must learn to enjoy each another, and the joy of being with your mate gives you the fun in marriage. Would you rather enjoy being married or just be married? The dress code for marriage is first dressing in God and being clothed in righteousness. Once we master this, we can then master our marriage in pleasing our mate in areas only we can please them. The dress code the church sometimes gives us is what they want you to have and not what is desired. People can have you in so many boxes that you think you are doing right with your marriage. To be honest, you will be in bondage to the people and your marriage failing. No one should tell you how to sex your spouse. No one should tell you how to dress for your spouse. Jesus leads, and the spouse proceeds. Don't let people put you in a box, but allow yourself to be in a dress code of sweet love.

# MARRIED BEFORE AND HURT

This chapter is one that will open the eyes of many because, unfortunately, many people are still hurting from a previous marriage. I am a witness of this because when I married my second husband in the '90s, I had some stuff still in me that was not of God. It was hurt that did not get healed. Some of you may not know, but I was married and divorced before. I tried, y'all. I did everything a woman could do, but that was not the husband God had for me. The moment I came into grips of that and not trying to make things happen, I had to be still and know that God was God in my situation (Psalms 46:10). I have seen this in so many churches: women take a bruise and let a man beat them because they think they are in love. Love is not punches, love is not negative words, love does not need you to feel lower, but love is knowing you love each other. When you love someone, you don't abuse them. You love them through the storm. We have an epidemic in the church where we think we are to stay with someone because we are married. The church has taught us wrong. We are married to the Lord first, and then we get married to who God has us to marry. I know the Asian church sets their children with who they should marry, but don't we do the same in America. Once we get in a church, we try to tell the saved youth who they should marry and who they should not. Yes, we want to set up the saved couple, not knowing they may not marry the person God desires them to marry. We must stop this because it is not of God. It is not important that you get married but that we marry who God wants us to marry. I believe we have not served those who have married and now are divorced. I am not saying all marriages in the church, but some of them are done this way. When problems come, we tell the couple they cannot divorce, and they must stay together. I believe in staying together once married, but I don't believe in staying together when the couple is fighting and hurting themselves.

Deciding to get married again is a great thing. Please do not allow anyone to hold you in and say you cannot be married. You can be happily married, and you can stand on God's promises for your life. Before you get married, you must make sure that you are totally healed from all hurts. If you are not healed in every area, you will know it because the man or woman you marry will press your button. When I got married to my husband I have been married to for more than twenty years, he pressed some buttons. He was not purposely doing it, but it was something that made me grow. I am so thankful that I received my healing. The Bible speaks of healing being the children's bread. I am healed from everything and anything marred that would hold my marriage in bondage.

We must not marry and have not been healed because it will damage what we already have. I am assured and confident in all things that God has for me is blessed and golden.

DECLARATION OVER HEALING

I DECLARE OVER YOU YOU WILL NOT BE DEFEATED, BUT YOU WILL BE IN A PLACE OF BEING HEALED AND STAYING HEALED. THERE IS NOTHING MISSING IN YOU OR BROKEN IN YOU. GOD IS WELL PLEASED WITH YOU, AND YOU DO NOT NEED TO THINK ANY LESS OF YOURSELF. IT IS YOUR SEASON, AND IT IS YOUR TIME TO BE HAPPILY MARRIED AND ENJOY THE BEST DAYS OF YOUR LIFE IN JESUS'S NAME.

# WHEN MARRIAGE
# IS NOT FUN

It has been said that a marriage is the way you make it. If you are married, I want you to think about that. It's not who you marry, but it's what your goals are before you get married. Honestly, I just wanted to be happily married. I wanted to be the one in my family who would be like my grandmother and could say I would be married for sixty-five years.

Well, that did not work out for me. I had been through a bad relationship, and God helped me overcome that storm. I freed myself from that ordeal, and it got me where I am now.

So I ended up divorcing my first husband. My slogan was all men are dogs, and I would never marry again, but I met a man named Joe Kirk Jr. from Atlanta, Georgia, and he changed my entire life. He did not come with sweet words. He came to me saying the Lord told him I was supposed to be his wife, and I could not believe it. I met a man, but then I kind of had a red flag because he was a believer of Jesus Christ, so of course, I thought he come like my ex-husband did. He was totally the opposite. He was to be a blessing to me. He was to be a blessing to my daughter whom I had out of wedlock. He was the answer to what I thought would never happen to me. Who was I? A mere yellow girl from North Carolina who was divorced and had a child from another man. The moment I met him, I knew there was something about him. He had this glow in his eyes that stimulated me and this softness of love that motivated me. There were times I gave him a hard time. I wanted him to work for what he was getting because I was a golden investment with a child in the package. Sometimes when you meet people, you can't give them all they want. You have to make them work for it. Believe me, all things were working for my good because he never stopped pursuing me. He was very persistent in all that he did. He would meet me at restaurants only to let me know he wanted to read the Bible to my daughter. I watched him like a hammer hitting a nail to make sure he was who he said he was. Joe would always bring me flowers and give me Liz Claiborne clothes. You see, back then, I was into wearing long dresses to my ankle because I attended the Holiness Church, and that was what they taught me. I found out it was not in the clothes quickly after marrying J. He would always share with me the word of God. Man looks at the outward appearance, but God looks at your heart. This made feel good because coming from a holiness background, it was not easy. I truly thought marriage was never to happen again for me because of the beating with words of being a divorcee. I came to understand the word more after marrying J. He helped me see more than just religion but a relationship with God. He helped get to know who I was and how much God loved me in spite of what I was facing.

Although I thought the fun of marriage was never to become my life, I found out in marrying Joe that there was still hope for me. Failed marriage, failed life, and raising a child out of wedlock, but God said, "I love you, Shonda."

That's all that matters. Don't ever look at your life as nothing. God is wonderful at making misfits into minds of productivity. He never gives up on us. God is what we need when we feel we have messed up our life. It's not about what you don't but what are you willing to do to correct it. When it's all said and done about life, there was no fun for me in marriage. It was just a day-to-day thing. I hated being married before Joe. I hated life because it felt more as a chore. I can proudly say marriage is not a chore. It is the love of Jesus shedding on every problem we may face. We face it together, and we make our life better together. Choose to make good choices that you will live with for the rest of your life. If you do not make these best choices, your life will be still and stuck in place.

Marriage is fun, but it is definitely what you make it.

LET ME PRAY FOR YOU. REPEAT AFTER ME.

FATHER GOD, FORGIVE ME OF ALL BAD DECISIONS. WASH MY MIND AND ALL THAT IS CONNECTED TO MY PAST THAT WANTS ME TO FAIL. LORD, I COME TO YOU IN FAITH, BELIEVING YOU ARE A LIFE-CHANGING GOD. TODAY I CONFESS THAT THE HANDS OF GOD ARE UPON ME, AND THE HEALING POWER OF JESUS CHRIST IS MOVING IN MY LIFE 'TIL THIS DAY FORWARD AND FOREVERMORE. I SPEAK LIFE OVER MY LIFE. I AM WHO GOD SAYS I AM, AND I CAN DO WHAT GOD SAYS I CAN DO, AND I HAVE WHAT GOD SAYS I HAVE. I AM NOT A DOUBTER BUT A BELIEVER OF JESUS CHRIST, AND MY LIFE IS BETTER IN JESUS'S NAME! AMEN. AMEN. AMEN.

# WHAT DOES THE MAN SAY ABOUT MARRIAGE

A man must look to be freed from pride. This trait is engraved on our subconscious to show self-worth, but it is a danger to the marriage if it expands to selfishness. The man can't be the sole deliverer of Christian traits in the home. And once a husband understands that he can depend on the wife to help in family decisions, the merrier the marriage becomes. When men take obedience in the Bible to say they are dictators in the home, you will end up going the same route as true-to-life dictatorships have gone, toppled in chaos and alone. Marriage is good when both are listening, looking, and acting on the needs of their mate.

My wife says this all the time: When I wake up, I should get up to see what I can do to please my mate.

This is good advice. Sometimes I fail, and at times I meet the need, but every day get this thought in your head. Every day you become a practical husband, able to meet the required work when needed and being a pillar for your wife when she needs it.

Sacrifice is spoken often in the Bible, and many would do well following Christ as he took action to demonstrate his sacrifice for our sins. When I am faced with a shortcoming, I must look at the fruits of the spirit and check off one by one each of them to see if I fell short of completely pleasing my wife. Limited in the prayer and word, a man can get deeply frustrated with a relationship with his wife because he lacks all the tools afforded to him by the word of God. And he becomes isolated because he lacks that intimacy with God. A strong word life and a spiritual relationship with God will show a man what is broken in his fruit box. I will call it, to fix if he lacking in love, joy, peace, longsuffering, gentleness, goodness, faith. When a real man has the spiritual walk in line, his natural relationship with his wife is working for God's glory and in his grace.

# MARRIED AND HAVING FUN!

There are different ways to have fun in marriage. The church has made us not have fun while we are married because of man-made rules. The church is not the sheriff of heaven, but God is the one who rules our lives. Marriage is not where we go to church or who is our pastor. Marriage is a beautiful thing between a man and a woman who love each other and enjoy each other. It is not a man and man or a woman and woman together, but the beauty of marriage is, from the beginning of time, in God's word. The Bible specifically says God made man and woman to be fruitful and multiply.

The greatest problem in marriage is when we allow and let in people who are not supposed to be in the marriage. This happens because we want everyone in our lives to have a voice in our marriage. Marriage is what we make it, but when we include voices that should not be in it, it makes problems inside the marriage. The Bible says leave and cleave, not marry and open the door for everyone to come in. Your parents should not be in your marriage, sharing what they think you should do, but you should make decisions that are best for both of you. When we involve parents, sometimes they take sides, and this makes problems in our marriages even more. Lesson no. 1: Keep people out of your marriage to have fun in your marriage. Married couples must decide not to allow anyone who would try to control their marriage.

Marriage is a wonderful thing, but are we wanting to stay in fun places? What do I mean? In my marriage, I have to work at being fun and appreciate who I am having fun with. Having fun in marriage and entertaining each other is a must. It causes you not only to learn about each other but also get to know each other. We should not get married and dry up like a desert. Most marriages have failed because of the simple fact that people have their thought patterns mixed up. What do I mean? We think marriage should be this way or that way and not God's way. God's way is not a bad way or a way of control. Marriage is not based on hearsay but on what God says. Marriage is not based on what a book with ten steps can teach you, but you will learn as you go.

One of the rewards of marriage is having a person God grants you that will lower their life and put your life on the line. I have seen my grandparents be married over sixty years, and they had some ups and downs, but they stuck it through. They had some awesome times. They taught me some things I need now. I am a military wife who have traveled all over the world. I miss my family and felt times of depression, but I kept being that faithful wife and caring mother. It is not easy when you have one parent present in the home. It is not easy when you have two parents in the home. The grace of God helps you balance everything you may face in your home, job, and other things you need to accomplish.

When it comes to the family unit, marriage lesson no. 2, never let your children have rule over your marriage. Let them know who are in control, and they should follow. Marriages that merge children by other mates into the family may have a problem. Some of the biggest problems are they do not get to know one another and there are no boundaries. Children need to know boundaries, no matter who they are and how old they are. If there is no boundaries, situations that could be avoided will arise. Communication is a big thing when it comes to relationships. Once the families are on board with communication, this will help all small fires not become blazes.

The third lesson highlighted in marriage is learning to celebrate life with each other when all hell is breaking loose. There are times you will feel as if, "Am I really supposed to be married to this person?"

Yes, you are, and you know it, but you are going through some challenges that normal couples go through in their marriage. The only difference with you and them is they may not have God and you have God in your lives. When we invite God in our marriage, this means we allow him to show us through his word people of like faith, and His Holy Spirit directs us on what he desires versus what we desire.

Many people do not know how to have fun in their marriage because they do not look beyond the spiritual part of being married. I like to hang out with my husband, walking on the streets of Vegas, shopping, riding a boat, and eating food I have never eaten. Marriage is built by two people coming to live together forever and making it work no matter what. Ladies, we cannot just leave a man because he leaves his socks in the floor or maybe he does not know how to clean a house. Men, you can't leave a woman because she doesn't know how to cook or take care of the house. I truly believe some of these things should be discussed before marriage is introduced. This is vital because expectations that are not spoken of can be a big deal.

I think the most fun times of my marriage with my husband is when we be adventurous and plan places we want to go. It is amazing because we always have fun doing some out-of-state things in other countries, and trying new foods is our thing. I like to see the expression on his face when he doesn't want the food but tries it because of me. It's the facial expression for me! We always go to places in America, Africa, London, Japan, etc. If you are married, getting away is a great thing to do. You can't always think new things can come from being in the same place all the time. New places open up new things.

Expect to do something new in your marriage, and God will help you enjoy marriage and have fun!

Printed in the United States
by Baker & Taylor Publisher Services